The ESSE

MACROECONOMICS II

Robert S. Rycroft, Ph.D.

Chairperson of Economics Department
Mary Washington College, Fredericksburg, VA

This book is a continuation of *"THE ESSENTIALS OF MACROECONOMICS I"* and begins with Chapter 10. It covers the usual course outline of Macroeconomics II. Earlier/basic topics are covered in *"THE ESSENTIALS OF MACROECONOMICS I"*.

Research and Education Association
61 Ethel Road West
Piscataway, New Jersey 08854

THE ESSENTIALS® OF MACROECONOMICS II

Printed in the United States of America

Library of Congress Catalog Card Number 89-62086

International Standard Book Number 0–87891–719-5

Revised Printing, 1991

ESSENTIALS is a registered trademark of
Research and Education Association, Piscataway, New Jersey

WHAT "THE ESSENTIALS" WILL DO FOR YOU

This book is a review and study guide. It is comprehensive and it is concise.

It helps in preparing for exams, in doing homework, and remains a handy reference source at all times.

It condenses the vast amount of detail characteristic of the subject matter and summarizes the **essentials** of the field.

It will thus save hours of study and preparation time.

The book provides quick access to the important facts, principles, theorems, concepts, and equations in the field.

Materials needed for exams can be reviewed in summary form – eliminating the need to read and re-read many pages of textbook and class notes. The summaries will even tend to bring detail to mind that had been previously read or noted.

This "ESSENTIALS" book has been prepared by an expert in the field, and has been carefully reviewed to assure accuracy and maximum usefulness.

Dr. Max Fogiel
Program Director

CONTENTS

This book is a continuation of *"THE ESSENTIALS OF MACROECONOMICS I"* and begins with Chapter 10. It covers the usual course outline of Macroeconomics II. Earlier/basic topics are covered in *"THE ESSENTIALS OF MACROECONOMICS I"*.

Chapter No.   **Page No.**

THE INCOME-EXPENDITURE MODEL

Turning Say's Law on its head, the simple income-expenditure model essentially incorporates the idea that "demand creates its own supply." Consequently, the level of spending, or aggregate expenditure (AE), is a major focus. Much of the analysis is directed toward analyzing the levels of the various types of spending:

$$AE = C + I + G + (X - M)$$

where C is consumption, I is investment, G is government spending, and $(X - M)$ is net exports (X is exports and M is imports).

10.1 CONSUMPTION SPENDING

Household Consumption Schedule—The household consumption schedule shows the relationship between a household's disposable income and its consumption spending. Increases in a household's disposable income should cause increases in its consumption spending.

Household Savings Schedule—The household savings schedule shows the relationship between a household's disposable income and its savings. Increases in a household's disposable income should cause increases in its savings.

Break-even Level—All income is consumed at the break-even level. There is no savings. At levels of income lower than break-even, the household is dissaving. Households can do this over short periods of times by drawing down on assets.

Average Propensity to Consume (APC)—The proportion of income consumed.

$$APC = C/DI$$

Average Propensity to Save (APS)—The proportion of income saved.

$$APS = S/DI$$

$$APC + APS = 1$$

The proportion of income consumed plus the proportion saved must equal 100%.

Marginal Propensity to Consume (MPC)—The proportion of additional income consumed.

$$MPC = \Delta C/\Delta DI$$

Marginal Propensity to Save (MPS)—The proportion of additional income saved.

$$MPS = \Delta S/\Delta DI$$

$$MPC + MPS = 1$$

The proportion of additional income consumed plus the proportion saved must equal 100%.

DI	C	S	APC	APS	MPC	MPS
10000	12000	−2000	1.20	−0.20	−	−
12000	13500	−1500	1.13	−0.13	0.75	0.25
14000	15000	−1000	1.07	−0.07	0.75	0.25
16000	16500	−500	1.03	−0.03	0.75	0.25
18000	18000	0	1.00	0.00	0.75	0.25
20000	19500	500	0.98	0.03	0.75	0.25
22000	21000	1000	0.95	0.05	0.75	0.25
24000	22500	1500	0.94	0.06	0.75	0.25
26000	24000	2000	0.92	0.08	0.75	0.25
28000	25500	2500	0.91	0.09	0.75	0.25

TABLE 10.1–Household Consumption and Savings Schedules

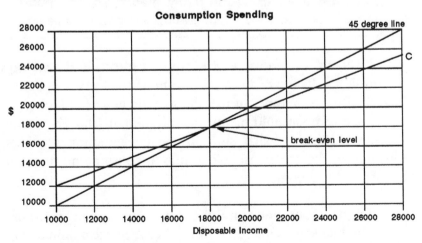

FIGURE 10.1–Household Consumption Schedule

84

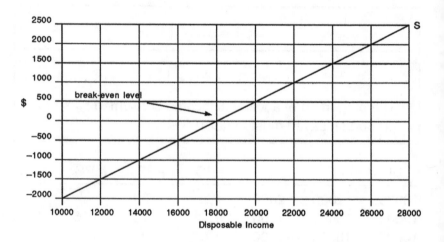

FIGURE 10.2–Household Savings Schedule

---

45 degree line

A 45 degree line bisects a graph quadrant forming an angle of 45 degrees with both the horizontal and vertical axes. Any point on a 45 degree line represents equal horizontal and vertical distances. Forty-five degree lines are included in many graphs used in economics because they make reading the graph easier.

Shifts in the household consumption and savings schedules —The schedules will shift due to changes in household thriftiness, number of members in the household, changes in the age of household members, and the household's wealth. An upward (downward) shift in the consumption (savings) schedule means the household wants to consume more out of its disposable income.

National Consumption Schedule—The national consumption schedule shows the relationship between the national level of disposable income and the national level of consumption.

Note the similarity between the national and household schedules.

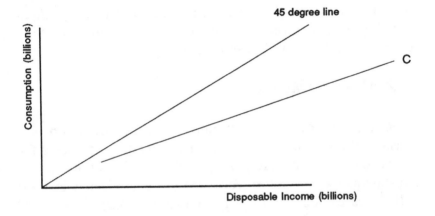

FIGURE 10.3–National Consumption Schedule

National Savings Schedule—The national savings schedule shows the relationship between the national level of disposable income and the national level of savings. Note the similarity between the national and household schedules.

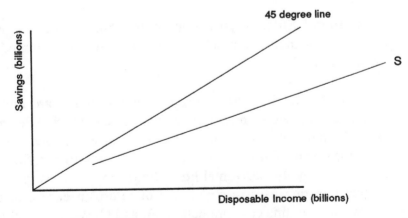

FIGURE 10.4–National Savings Schedule

Shifts in the national consumption and savings schedules—The schedules will shift due to changes in national thriftiness, interest rates, the price level, and national wealth. An upward (downward) shift in the consumption (savings) schedule indicates that consumers wish to consume more (save less) out of a given level of disposable income.

10.2 INVESTMENT

Rate of return on investment—The rate of return is a measure of the profitability of an investment. It compares the profits earned on an investment with the size of the initial investment. Rate of return formulas are complicated in most realistic cases. For an investment that will last forever and return the same profit every year, the formula is:

---

rate of return = (annual profit)/(investment)

For example, if a $10 million factory will earn a profit of $1 million a year forever, then the rate of return is $1 million/$10 million = 10%.

Marginal Efficiency of Investment (MEI)—The marginal efficiency of investment schedule shows the rate of return on the last dollar invested.

Firm's MEI Schedule—Projects A through E are ranked by (expected) rate of return. The width of each rectangle indicates the amount of investment required for each. The interest rate (measuring the opportunity cost of funds to the firm) is represented by the horizontal line. The firm will invest in every project that promises to pay a rate of return in excess of the interest rate, in this case projects A, B, and C. Were the interest rate to fall (downward shift in interest rate line), more projects might become worthwhile. If the interest rate rises, the firm might invest in fewer projects.

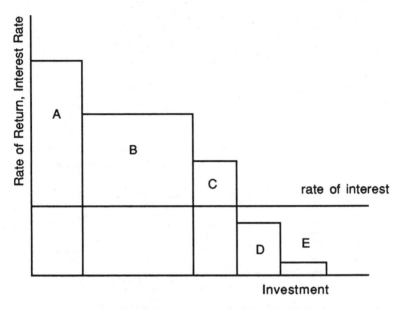

FIGURE 10.5–Firm's MEI Schedule

Economy's MEI Schedule—For the economy as a whole, there are so many projects that the MEI schedule becomes a smooth curve. The economy's level of investment is determined by the intersection of the MEI schedule and the rate of interest. Increases in the rate of interest will reduce investment spending; decreases will raise investment spending.

Shifts in the MEI schedule—The MEI schedule will shift as a result in changes in:

1. expected product demand

2. technology and innovation

3. cost of new capital goods

4. corporate income tax rates

88

Factors causing firms to want to invest more at any interest rate will shift the MEI curve outward/upward/rightward. Factors causing firms to want to invest less at any interest rate will shift the MEI curve inward/downward/leftward.

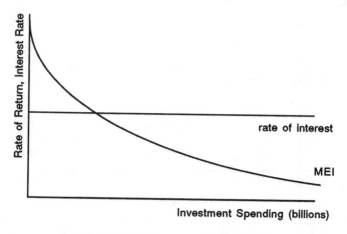

FIGURE 10.6–Economy's MEI Schedule

10.3 GOVERNMENT SPENDING

The level of government spending is determined by allocational, distributional, and stabilization needs. Allocational needs reflect society's views of the proper level of spending for public and merit goods. Distributional needs reflect society's views of equity regarding the distribution of income. Stabilization needs reflect society's view of the proper level of spending to achieve unemployment, inflation, and economic growth goals. Economists have not gone much beyond this very general statement in analyzing the level of government spending.

10.4 NET EXPORTS

Americans' willingness to purchase foreign goods and services (import) is influenced by their income and the relative price of the goods and services. At higher levels of income, Americans will purchase more of all goods and services, including those produced abroad. When the prices of foreign goods and services fall relative to domestic goods and services, more foreign goods and services will be demanded.

Foreign export demand is similarly determined.

10.5 EQUILIBRIUM IN A CLOSED PRIVATE ECONOMY

Assumptions of the model—A closed, private economy is one with no international trade and no government. Hence, the expression for Aggregate Expenditure is that shown in the box. The level of investment is autonomous. The price level is fixed.

$$AE = C + I$$

Autonomous Spending—Spending is autonomous if its level is not influenced by the level of income. It may be influenced by other factors.

Induced Spending—Spending is induced if its level is influenced by the level of income.

Inventory change—In the simple model, inventory change refers to unexpected increases or decreases in firms' inventory holdings. This happens when firms incorrectly anticipate what the market will be willing to buy.

THREE WAYS TO IDENTIFY EQUILIBRIUM

1. **AE equal to GNP** indicates a point of equilibrium. If AE >

GNP	C	S	I	AE	Inventory Change	Condition of Economy
3500	3125	375	500	3625	-125	expand
3600	3200	400	500	3700	-100	expand
3700	3275	425	500	3775	-75	expand
3800	3350	450	500	3850	-50	expand
3900	3425	475	500	3925	-25	expand
4000	3500	500	500	4000	0	equilibrium
4100	3575	525	500	4075	25	contract
4200	3650	550	500	4150	50	contract
4300	3725	575	500	4225	75	contract
4400	3800	600	500	4300	100	contract

TABLE 10.2–Equilibrium in a Closed, Private Economy

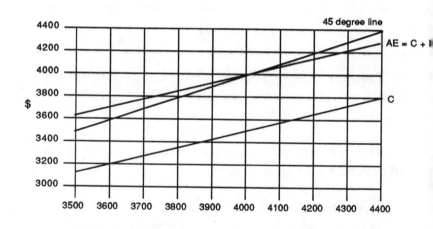

FIGURE 10.7–Equilibrium in a Closed, Private Economy

GNP, then current production is insufficient to satisfy demand. Firms may be forced to draw down on their inventories. Firms will respond to this situation by hiring more resources and expanding production. If AE < GNP, firms

91

cannot sell all their current production. Unsold goods will be placed in inventory causing firms to reduce production in layoff resources. If AE = GNP, then current production is just adequate to satisfy demand. There is no reason to expand or reduce production so there is equilibrium.

2. **S = I** indicates a point of equilibrium. If I > S then current production is insufficient to satisfy demand, and the economy will expand. If I < S, then current production exceeds demand, and the economy will contract.

3. Equilibrium is also found where **inventory change is 0.** If inventory change is negative, current production was inadequate to meet demand so inventories were drawn down leading firms to expand production to satisfy demand and rebuild inventories. If inventory change is positive, current production exceeded demand and the excess was placed in inventory leading firms to reduce production.

10.6 THE MULTIPLIER

The Multiplier Principle—Increases in autonomous spending will cause GNP to increase by a multiple of the initial increase in spending. Intuitively, suppose business increases its spending for investment goods. This will increase incomes in the investment goods industries by an equivalent amount. Out of this new income, the employees and owners of the investment goods industries will be able to increase their own consumption. This spending raises income in the consumption goods industries. The owners and employees of the consumptions goods industries will then be able to increase their spending which will raise income and spending elsewhere in the economy. In short, additional spending raises incomes which leads to additional spending which raises incomes still more which leads to further spending which raises incomes, and so on.

Investment multiplier—The investment multiplier measures how much GNP will be created by an additional dollar of autonomous investment. In the example (Table 10.3 and Figure 10.8), an increase in investment of 25 caused the equilibrium level of GNP to rise by 100. Therefore, the investment multiplier was $\Delta GNP/ \Delta I = 4$. In a simple income-expenditure model the formula for the investment multiplier is $1/(1-MPC)$. To compute the effect of additional investment on GNP use the following formula:

$$\Delta I \times 1/(1-MPC) = \Delta GNP$$

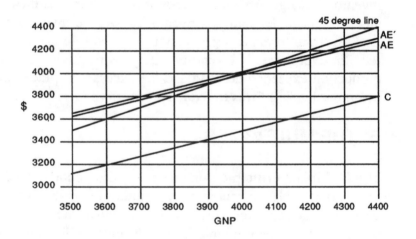

FIGURE 10.8–The Investment Multiplier

Consumption multiplier—The consumption multiplier measures how much GNP will be created by an additional dollar of autonomous consumption. In the example (Table 10.4 and Figure 10.9), an increase in autonomous consumption of 25 caused the equilibrium level of GNP to rise by 100. Therefore, the consumption multiplier is $\Delta GNP/\Delta C = 4$.

In a simple income-expenditure model the formula for the

GNP	C	S	I	I′	AE	AE′	Inventory Change	Inventory Change′
3500	3125	375	500	525	3625	3650	−125	−150
3600	3200	400	500	525	3700	3725	−100	−125
3700	3275	425	500	525	3775	3800	−75	−100
3800	3350	450	500	525	3850	3875	−50	−75
3900	3425	475	500	525	3925	3950	−25	−50
4000	3500	500	500	525	4000	4025	0	−25
4100	3575	525	500	525	4075	4100	25	0
4200	3650	550	500	525	4150	4175	50	25
4300	3725	575	500	525	4225	4250	75	50
4400	3800	600	500	525	4300	4325	100	75

TABLE 10.3–Investment Multiplier

consumption multiplier is $1/(1-MPC)$. To compute the effect of additional consumption on GNP use the following formula:

$$\Delta C \times 1/(1-MPC) = \Delta GNP$$

GNP	C	S	C′	S′	I	AE	AE′	Inventory Change	Inventory Change′
3500	3125	375	3150	350	500	3625	3650	−125	−150
3600	3200	400	3225	375	500	3700	3725	−100	−125
3700	3275	425	3300	400	500	3775	3800	−75	−100
3800	3350	450	3375	425	500	3850	3875	−50	−75
3900	3425	475	3450	450	500	3925	3950	−25	−50
4000	3500	500	3525	475	500	4000	4025	0	−25
4100	3575	525	3600	500	500	4075	4100	25	0
4200	3650	550	3675	525	500	4150	4175	50	25
4300	3725	575	3750	550	500	4225	4250	75	50
4400	3800	600	3825	575	500	4300	4325	100	75

TABLE 10.4–Consumption Multiplier

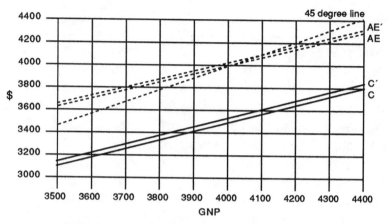

FIGURE 10.9–The Consumption Multiplier

10.7 MACROECONOMIC PROBLEMS

Potential GNP—Potential GNP is the amount of output the economy is capable of producing at full employment. In the Keynesian model, there is nothing automatically pushing the economy toward potential GNP.

Recessionary Gap—Insufficient spending will lead the economy to an equilibrium below potential GNP. The recessionary gap measures the shortfall in aggregate expenditure. In Figure 10.10, potential GNP = 4100. The level of spending is AE. AE′ is the level needed to achieve potential. The gap is the vertical distance between AE and AE′ at potential GNP. The gap represents the Keynesian idea that recessions are caused by too little spending, and that more spending is the solution.

Inflationary Gap—Too much spending will lead the economy to an equilibrium above potential GNP. Since the economy is not capable of producing more than its potential for extended periods of time, what must happen is that the average price level must rise. The inflationary gap measures the excess

95

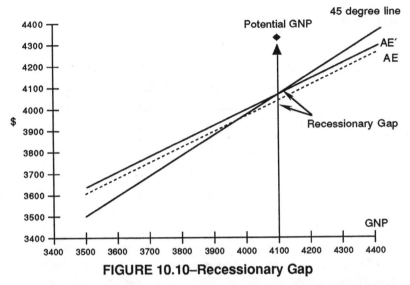

FIGURE 10.10–Recessionary Gap

in aggregate expenditure. In Figure 10.11, potential GNP = 3900. AE is the level of spending. Note AE exceeds GNP at potential. AE´ is the level of spending that would not put upward pressure on prices. The gap is the vertical distance between AE and AE´ at potential GNP. The gap represents the Keynesian idea that inflation is caused by too much spending, and that reducing spending is the solution.

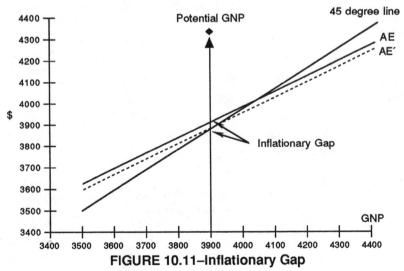

FIGURE 10.11–Inflationary Gap

96

10.8 FISCAL POLICY

Equilibrium in a model with a government sector—
When government is allowed in the model:

$$AE = C + I + G$$

$$DI = GNP - T$$

Taxes are a complicating factor because they can affect both households and firms. In the simplest model, the assumption made is that taxes are of the lump-sum variety and are levied only on households.

GNP	T	DI	C	I	G	AE	Inventory Change
3500	1000	2500	1900	500	1200	3600	−100
3600	1000	2600	1980	500	1200	3680	−80
3700	1000	2700	2060	500	1200	3760	−60
3800	1000	2800	2140	500	1200	3840	−40
3900	1000	2900	2220	500	1200	3920	−20
4000	1000	3000	2300	500	1200	4000	0
4100	1000	3100	2380	500	1200	4080	20
4200	1000	3200	2460	500	1200	4160	40
4300	1000	3300	2540	500	1200	4240	60
4400	1000	3400	2620	500	1200	4320	80

TABLE 10.5–Equilibrium in a Closed Economy with Simple Government Sector

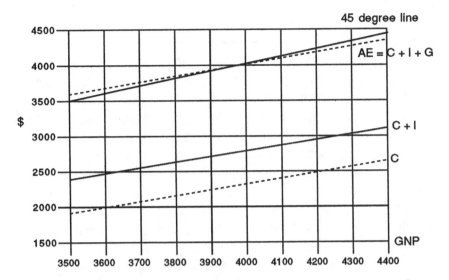

FIGURE 10.12–Equilibrium in a Closed Economy with Simple Government Sector

THREE WAYS TO FIND EQUILIBRIUM:

Like the simpler model, there are three ways to find equilibrium. The conditions AE = GNP and Inventory change = 0 are unchanged. The S = I condition is replaced by the slightly more complicated

$$S + T = I + G$$

Government Spending Multiplier—The government spending multiplier measures how much GNP will be created by a dollar of government spending. In the example (Table 10.6 and Figure 10.13), an increase in G of 20 causes GNP to rise by 100. The government spending multiplier is ΔGNP/ΔG = 5. The formula is government spending multiplier = 1/(1–MPC), where the MPC is calculated as C/GNP. To compute the impact of government spending on GNP use:

$$\Delta G \times 1/(1–MPC) = GNP$$

GNP	T	DI	C	I	G	G´	AE	AE´
3500	1000	2500	1900	500	1200	1220	3600	3620
3600	1000	2600	1980	500	1200	1220	3680	3700
3700	1000	2700	2060	500	1200	1220	3760	3780
3800	1000	2800	2140	500	1200	1220	3840	3860
3900	1000	2900	2220	500	1200	1220	3920	3940
4000	1000	3000	2300	500	1200	1220	4000	4020
4100	1000	3100	2380	500	1200	1220	4080	4100
4200	1000	3200	2460	500	1200	1220	4160	4180
4300	1000	3300	2540	500	1200	1220	4240	4260
4400	1000	3400	2620	500	1200	1220	4320	4340

TABLE 10.6–Government Spending Multiplier

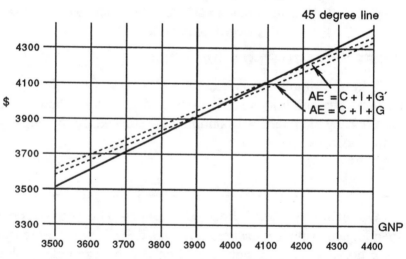

FIGURE 10.13–Government Spending Multiplier

Tax Multiplier—The tax multiplier measures how much GNP will be reduced by a dollar in additional taxes. Intuitively, when taxes are raised, consumer disposable income is reduced. This will reduce consumption spending leading to a multiplied decrease in GNP. In the example (Table 10.7 and Figure 10.14),

99

an increase in T of 25 will reduce C by 20 ($\Delta T \times MPC$), where the MPC is defined as $\Delta C/\Delta DI$. The reduced C will cause GNP to fall by 100. The tax multiplier is $\Delta GNP/\Delta T = -4$. The formula for the tax multiplier is $-MPC/(1-MPC)$, where the MPC is defined as $\Delta C/\Delta GNP$. To compute the impact of tax increases on GNP, use:

$$\Delta T \times -MPC/(1-MPC) = \Delta GNP$$

Balanced Budget Multiplier—The balanced budget multiplier measures how much GNP will be created by a dollar increase in both G and T (maintaining the current budget balance). Intuitively, the increase in G will raise GNP by a multiple amount. The increase in T will reduce GNP by a multiple amount, but the net effect will be positive because government spending has a stronger stimulative effect than taxes have dampening effect. This is because tax changes do not translate dollar for dollar into consumption cuts. Saving absorbs some of the change. From th chart (Table 10.8), an increase in G and T of

GNP	T	T′	DI	DI′	C	C′	I	G	AE	AE′
3500	1000	1025	2500	2475	1900	1880	500	1200	3600	3580
3600	1000	1025	2600	2575	1980	1960	500	1200	3680	3660
3700	1000	1025	2700	2675	2060	2040	500	1200	3760	3740
3800	1000	1025	2800	2775	2140	2120	500	1200	3840	3820
3900	1000	1025	2900	2875	2220	2200	500	1200	3920	3900
4000	1000	1025	3000	2975	2300	2280	500	1200	4000	3980
4100	1000	1025	3100	3075	2380	2360	500	1200	4080	4060
4200	1000	1025	3200	3175	2460	2440	500	1200	4160	4140
4300	1000	1025	3300	3275	2540	2520	500	1200	4240	4220
4400	1000	1025	3400	3375	2620	2600	500	1200	4320	4300

TABLE 10.7–Tax Multiplier

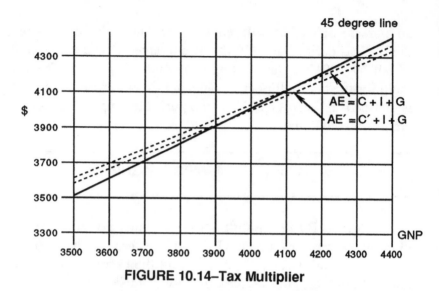

FIGURE 10.14–Tax Multiplier

100 will cause GNP to increase by 100. The balanced budget multiplier is equal to 1. To compute the impact of a balanced budget increase on GNP use:

$$\Delta B \times 1 = \Delta GNP, \text{ where } \Delta B = \Delta G = \Delta T$$

GNP	T	T′	DI	DI′	C	C′	I	G	G′	AE	AE′
3500	1000	1100	2500	2400	1900	1820	500	1200	1300	3600	3620
3600	1000	1100	2600	2500	1980	1900	500	1200	1300	3680	3700
3700	1000	1100	2700	2600	2060	1980	500	1200	1300	3760	3780
3800	1000	1100	2800	2700	2140	2060	500	1200	1300	3840	3860
3900	1000	1100	2900	2800	2220	2140	500	1200	1300	3920	3940
4000	1000	1100	3000	2900	2300	2220	500	1200	1300	4000	4020
4100	1000	1100	3100	3000	2380	2300	500	1200	1300	4080	4100
4200	1000	1100	3200	3100	2460	2380	500	1200	1300	4160	4180
4300	1000	1100	3300	3200	2540	2460	500	1200	1300	4240	4260
4400	1000	1100	3400	3300	2620	2540	500	1200	1300	4320	4340

TABLE 10.8–Balanced Budget Multiplier

CHAPTER 11

FISCAL POLICY ISSUES

11.1 STABILIZATION POLICY

Discretionary Fiscal Policy—Discretionary fiscal policy refers to changes in government spending and taxes consciously made by the government to achieve certain stabilization goals. For example, if the economy threatens to head into a recession, and the government makes a decision to cut taxes to maintain purchasing power, that is a discretionary action.

Automatic Stabilizers—The level of spending of some government programs is automatically influenced by the state of the economy. For example, when unemployment goes up, government spending for unemployment compensation automatically increases. In a similar manner, the revenue received from most forms of taxes is also influenced by the economy. For example, personal income tax collections fall during recessions as wages drop and people lose their jobs. Thus during recessions, automatically government spending rises and tax collections fall. During periods of full or near-full employment (when inflation dangers are greatest), automatically government spending falls and tax collections rise. Both sets of actions are what the theory of fiscal policy would call for in those situations. These economy-sensitive programs are called automatic stabilizers because they automatically work to stabilize the economy. As a general rule, automatic stabilizers cannot cure recessions or inflation, but make the problem less severe than it otherwise would be.

The Budget Cycle—During the period January through September, the President proposes a budget and Congress accepts, amends, or rejects the proposals. The budget decided upon goes into effect on October 1 and remains in effect through the following September 30, a period known as the fiscal year. The budget process is a lengthy one, and deciding on a proper budget to meet the stabilization needs of the economy requires the ability to forecast accurately more than one year into the future, something economists are not good at. Many economists believe these considerations vitiate the effectiveness of fiscal policy as a stabilization tool.

Full Employment or Structural Budget—The full employment budget is an estimate of what government spending, taxes, and the deficit would be if the economy were at full employment. Its purpose is to get a better picture of how expansionary or contractionary the government's budget is. The problem with using actual spending, tax, and deficit figures is that each of these factors is influenced by the state of the economy. For example, the government may enact an austere budget (limited spending and high taxes), yet if there is a recession, automatic stabilizers may lead to greater spending, lower taxes and a larger deficit, which would be a misleading picture of what the actual budget intended. By estimating spending, taxes, and the deficit at full employment, we remove the effect of the economy on the budget.

Functional Finance—Under a system of functional finance, government spending and taxes are set to meet the stabilization needs of the economy (run deficit during recession and surplus during inflation), with little concern given to the resulting deficit and surplus).

11.2 DEFICITS AND THE PUBLIC DEBT

Size of the Deficit and Public Debt—In calendar 1988, the U.S. Government ran a deficit of approximately $155 billion, leaving the U.S. Government with a debt of approximately $2.6 trillion at the end of 1988. Both are "big" numbers, but there are some considerations that put these numbers in perspective:

1. A significant portion of the debt, approximately $550 billion, was owed to agencies of the U.S. Government (Federal Reserve System, Social Security Trust Fund, etc.), leaving a net debt of approximately $2.1 trillion.

2. Only 13% of this net debt was owed to foreign nations, although this percentage has been growing in recent years (see discussion of Internal Debt below).

3. The burden of debt to an entity can only be properly assessed by comparing it to the entity's financial condition. Using a household analogy, a $20,000 debt is less burdensome to a household earning $150,000 per year than one earning $20,000. In the case of deficits and the debt, a useful comparison is with GNP. Figure 11.1 compares annual deficits with GNP. Recent deficit-to-GNP ratios have been higher than average, but there have been periods in our history when they have been even higher. Figure 11.2 shows the Debt-to-GNP ratio. Although this has risen in recent years, it remains considerably below the level at the end of World War II (a

war we won, while piling up huge amounts of debt). Figure 11.3 shows the ratio of interest payments on the debt to GNP, which tells a similar story to the two previous figures.

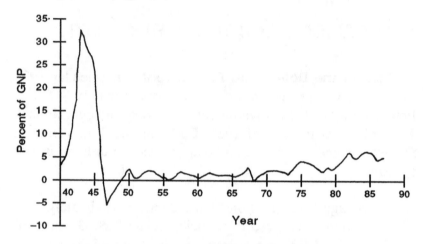

FIGURE 11.1–Trend in Deficit Relative to GNP

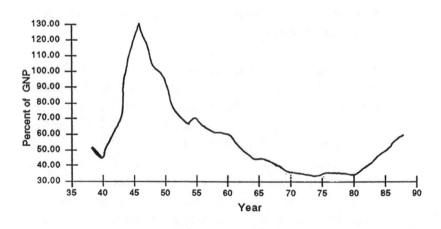

FIGURE 11.2–Trend in Debt Relative to GNP

Internal Debt—An internal debt is one we "owe to ourselves." If the debt issued by the government is purchased by Americans, then it is an internal debt. An internal debt is considered easier to maintain. Most of the debt of the U.S. government is an internal debt.

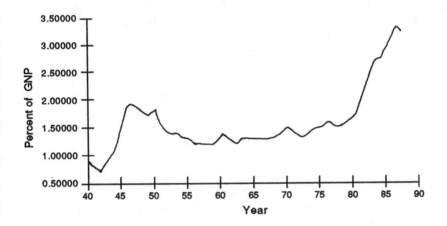

FIGURE 11.3–Trend in Interest Payments Relative to GNP

External Debt—An external debt is one we owe to an outside institution. External debts are considered more onerous than internal debts because to service and pay them back we must give up assets.

Refinancing the Debt—Most government (and corporate) debt is paid back by refinancing. This means that the government borrows from other sources to pay back the creditors whose loans have become due.

National Bankruptcy—Bankruptcy occurs when a unit is unable to pay its debts. This is unlikely to happen in the case of the United States. Since the debt is largely internal, we can simply tax ourselves to pay ourselves back. There may be dis-

106

tributional problems here. If worse came to worse, the government could simply print money.

Crowding Out—One of the generally agreed upon problems of the public debt is crowding out. This occurs when the public debt has the effect of reducing (or crowding out) private investment. At one level, we can say that the money the government borrows is no longer available to be borrowed by the private sector. At another level, government borrowing increases the demand for credit which raises interest rates. The higher interest rates crowd out private sector investment. If there is less investment, the economy will not grow as fast. Crowding out should only be a problem when the economy is at or near full employment. Also, if the government spending financed is used to produce valuable assets, the problem is reduced.

Deficits and Inflation—While budget deficits are frequently accused of being inflationary, the truth is a bit more complicated. Deficits can be inflationary, but it depends when they are incurred. Deficits occurring when the economy is at or near full employment can be inflationary because they can cause an inflationary gap situation. When the economy is operating well below potential, inflationary problems are unlikely, and deficits may be needed to get the economy moving again.

Gramm-Rudman-Hollings Balanced Budget Law—As a result of the huge budget deficits incurred during the Reagan Administration, Congress passed and the President signed the Gramm-Rudman-Hollings Balanced Budget Law in 1985. The law mandates that the government reduce the budget deficit to progressively smaller specified levels each year until the deficit is eliminated in 1991. In the event Congress and the President cannot agree on budget cuts, automatic spending cuts take place. Its economic wisdom aside, the law has two weaknesses. First, there is no mechanism to enforce automatic spending cuts. Second, the deficit targets are considered met if they are consistent with the government's economic forecast. If the forecast proves too optimistic, then the deficit targets will not be achieved.

CHAPTER 12

MONEY AND BANKING

12.1 WHAT MONEY IS AND DOES

Money—Money is anything that is **generally acceptable** in exchange for goods and services and in payment of debts. Suppose you had something you wanted to sell. Few would be willing to part with their product for a commodity like a loaf of bread, a chicken, or an automobile hubcap. All would be willing to exchange their product for coins, currency, or a check. Therefore, these latter items are money because they are generally acceptable. Everybody is willing to accept them in exchange for what they want to sell.

Functions of Money—Money performs four particular functions:

1. **Medium of Exchange**—Money is used to facilitate exchanges of goods and services. Money makes buying and selling easier. Assume we had an economy where nothing was money. Such an economy is known as a **barter economy**. In a barter economy goods and services exchange directly for other goods and services. If you want an axe

that someone is selling, you must find an item that person wants to trade for it. Barter requires a **double coincidence of wants**, each party must want what the other party has. If that condition does not hold, then exchange cannot take place, and valuable resources can be wasted in putting together trades. With money this problem never arises because **everyone always wants money**. Consequently, the resources used to facilitate exchanges can be put to more productive use.

2. **Unit of value**—We use our monetary unit as the standard measure of value. We say a shirt is worth $25.00, not 14 chickens.

3. **Store of Value**—Money is one of the forms wealth can be stored in. Alternatives include stocks and bonds, real estate, gold, great paintings, and many others. One advantage of storing wealth in money form is that money is the most **liquid** of all assets. **Liquidity** refers to the ease with which an asset can be transformed into spendable form. Money is already in spendable form. The disadvantage of holding wealth in money form is that money typically pays a lower return than other assets.

4. **Standard of Deferred Payment**—Money is used in transactions involving payments to be made at a future date. An example would be building contracts where full payment is made only when the project is completed. This function of money is implicit in the three already discussed.

What serves as money?—Virtually anything can and has served as money. Gold, silver, shells, boulders, cheap metal, paper, and electronic impulses stored in computers are examples of the varied forms money has taken. The only requirement is that the item be generally acceptable. Money does **not** have to

110

have intrinsic value (see below). Typically the items that have served as money have had the following additional characteristics[1]:

1. durability

2. divisibility

3. homogeneity (uniformity or standardization)

4. portability (high value-to-weight and value-to-volume)

5. relative stability of supply

6. optimal scarcity

What Makes Money Valuable?—Money is valuable if it can be used for or exchanged for something useful. Money's lack of intrinsic value means it cannot be used for anything useful. Why can it be exchanged for something useful? Sellers accept money because they know they can use it anywhere else in the country to buy goods and services and pay off debts. If they could not do that, they would not want it. What this means is that the substance that is used for money need not be valuable, and that money need not be backed by anything valuable. Such is the case. Our money is not backed by gold, silver, or anything else. It is just cheap metal, cheap paper, and electronic impulses stored in computers. Gold can be put to better use filling teeth!

12.2 THE UNITED STATES' MONEY SUPPLY

While there are many different definitions of the money supply available, the two most commonly used are M1 and M2.

---

1. Ralph T. Byrns and Gerald W. Stone, *Macroeconomics*, 3rd edition, (Scott, Foresman and Company, 1987), p. 228.

M1—M1 consists of currency, demand deposits, other checkable deposits, and traveler's checks.

Currency—coins and paper money.

Demand deposits—These are checking accounts held in commercial banks. Funds can be transferred from person to person by means of a check. Demand deposits are considered money because checks are generally acceptable.

Other checkable deposits—This category includes all other financial institution deposits upon which checks can be written. Among these are NOW accounts, ATS accounts, and credit union share drafts.

Traveler's checks—Most traveler's checks are generally acceptable throughout much of the world.

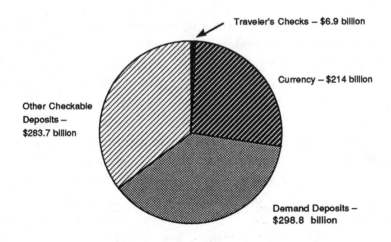

FIGURE 12.1–Composition of M1, Dec. 1989

M2—This definition includes all of M1 along with savings deposits, small denomination time deposits, money market mutual funds and deposit accounts, overnight Repo's, and Euro-dollars.

Savings Deposits—These are the common passbook savings accounts. They do not provide check writing privileges.

Small Denomination time deposits—A better-known name is certificates of deposits (CD's). They typically do not provide check writing privileges.

Money market mutual funds and deposit accounts—Both mutual funds and deposit accounts are investment funds. Large numbers of people pool their money to allow for diversification and professional investment management. Mutual funds are managed by private financial companies. Deposit accounts are managed by commercial banks. Investors earn a return on their investment and have limited check-writing privileges.

Overnight Repo's and Eurodollars—Overnight Repo's stand for overnight repurchase agreements. Essentially, these are short-term (overnight) loans. A corporation with excess cash may arrange to purchase a security from a bank with the stipulation that the bank will buy the security back the next day at a slightly higher price. The corporation receives a return on its money, and the bank gets access to funds. Eurodollars are dollar-denominated demand deposits held in banks outside the United States (not just in Europe). From the standpoint of M2, deposits held in Caribbean branches of Federal Reserve member banks are relevant. These deposits are easily accessed by U.S. residents. While both items are important in financial affairs, together they are a negligible proportion of M2.

A significant proportion of M2 cannot be used as a medium of exchange. Why, then, are the items considered money? First, each of these items is highly liquid. Second, studies indicate that people's economic behavior is not very sensitive to their relative holdings of the various assets in question.

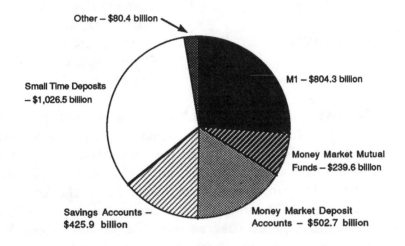

FIGURE 12.2–Composition of M2, Dec. 1988

12.3 THE FINANCIAL SYSTEM

Financial Intermediaries—Financial intermediaries are organizations such as commercial banks, savings and loan institutions, credit unions, and insurance companies. They play an important role in facilitating the saving and investment process which helps the economy grow. Savers typically look to place their money where the combination of return, liquidity, and safety is best. Through the various types of deposits they offer, financial intermediaries compete for the saved funds. The money so obtained is used to finance borrowing. Through their ability to obtain large pools of money from many depositors, intermediaries are able to service the needs of large borrowers.

Balance Sheet of Typical Bank

Assets	Liabilities
Reserves	Demand Deposits
Loans	Savings Deposits
Securities	Time Deposits
Property	Other Deposits
Other Assets	Net Worth

Reserves—Reserves are a bank's money holdings. Most reserves are held in the form of demand deposits at other banks or the Federal Reserve System (see 13.1). The remainder is cash in the bank's vault. Reserves are held to meet the demand for cash on the part of depositors, and to honor checks drawn upon the bank. The amount of reserves a bank must hold is based on the **required reserve ratio**. Set by the Federal Reserve System, the required reserve ratio is a number form 0 to 1.00 and determines the level of reserve holdings relative to the bank's deposits.

Required Reserves—Required reserves are the amount a bank is legally obligated to hold. Required reserves are calculated by multiplying the required reserve ratio by the amount of deposits.

Required Reserves = required reserve ratio × deposits

The required reserve ratio does not make banks safe. In the absence of a requirement, most banks would voluntarily hold adequate reserves to be "safe." In fact, the level of reserves banks are required to hold is probably higher than what they need to be safe. The main purpose of the requirement is to give the Federal Reserve System some control over the banks (see

13.1.4.b).

Excess Reserves—Excess reserves are the difference between the amount of reserves a bank holds and what it is required to hold.

All banks hold excess reserves at all times for reasons of financial prudence, however greater excess reserves will be held during periods of financial uncertainty.

> Excess Reserves = Reserves − Required Reserves

Why Can Banks Hold "Fractional" Reserves?—All banks constantly operate with reserve holdings only a fraction of deposit liabilities. This is known as **fractional reserve banking**. If all depositors tried to withdraw their money simultaneously, banks would not be able to honor the demands. Fortunately, this is unlikely to happen because people like to hold deposits because they are safe and convenient. On a normal business day, some withdrawals are made, but these are counterbalanced by new deposits. Reserve holdings need only be a small fraction of deposits for prudent operation.

12.4 THE MONEY CREATION PROCESS

Assume M1 consists of of currency and demand deposits only. The banking system consists of many small banks. The required reserve ratio is .20, and all banks are "loaned up" (no bank holds excess reserves). The balance sheet for a "typical" bank, Bank A, and the nation's money supply are shown below. Throughout let R = reserves, L = loans, DD = demand deposits, and NW = net worth.

	Bank A		Nation's Money Supply
R 10,000	DD 50,000	DD =	1,000,000
L 90,000	NW 50,000	Currency =	200,000
		M1 =	1,200,000

Assume an individual deposits $1,000 in cash in bank A. Note that the nation's money supply does not change, but its composition does.

	Bank A		Nation's Money Supply
R 11,000	DD 51,000	DD =	1,001,000
L 90,000	NW 50,000	Currency =	199,000
		M1 =	1,200,000

Bank A's required reserves are now $.20 \times 51,000 = 10,200$, meaning it has excess reserves of 800. It will move to lend out this money because excess reserves do not earn a return. Note that the nation's money supply will increase as a result of this.

	Bank A		Nation's Money Supply
R 11,000	DD 51,800	DD =	1,001,800
L 90,800	NW 50,000	Currency =	199,000
		M1 =	1,200,800

Presumably the money will be quickly spent and deposited in another bank, Bank B. Bank B will collect on the check from Bank A, frequently using the Federal Reserve System as intermediary.

After the check has cleared, the balance sheets of A and B will look as follows (Bank B's balance sheet only shows changes

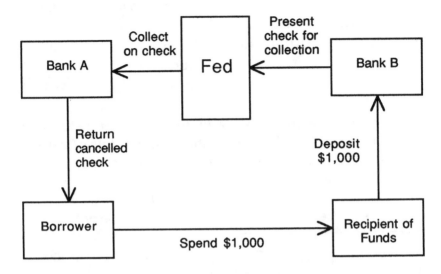

FIGURE 12.3–The Check Clearing Process

in the categories.) Note that check clearing will not affect the size of the nation's money supply, only which banks it is the liability of.

Bank A		Nation's Money Supply	
R 10,200	DD 51,000	DD =	1,001,800
L 90,800	NW 50,000	Currency =	199,000
		M1 =	1,200,800

Bank B	
R +800	DD + 800

Bank B now is holding excess reserves of 640, which it will move to lend out. This will cause the nation's money supply to increase by an additional 640.

Bank B	
R +800	DD +1,440
L +640	

Nation's Money Supply

DD =	1,002,400
Currency =	199,000
M1 =	1,201,440

Assuming the loan is spent by the writing of a check that the recipient deposits in Bank C, the balance sheets of Banks B and C will change as shown while the nation's money supply remains unchanged.

Bank B	
R +800	DD +800
L +640	

Nation's Money Supply

DD =	1,002,400
Currency =	199,000
M1 =	1,201,440

Bank C	
R +640	DD +640

Bank C is now holding excess reserves of 512 (can you calculate this amount?), which it will move to lend out. The nation's money supply will expand by the amount of the loan.

Bank C	
R +640	DD +1152
L +512	

Nation's Money Supply

DD =	1,002,952
Currency =	199,000
M1 =	1,201,952

The process will continue in a similar manner incorporating more and more banks (some banks may enter the process more than once). The chart summarizes the process:

Summary Chart

Bank	New Demand Deposits	New Required Reserves	New Loans	Cumulative New Demand Deposits (from second col.)
A	1000	200	800	1000
B	800	160	640	1800
C	640	128	512	2440
D	512	102.40	409.60	2952
All other banks	2048	409.60	1638.40	5000
Totals	5000	1000	4000	

An important conclusion is that the initial deposit of $1000 allowed the banking system to expand deposit liabilities by $5,000. The formula to calculate this is given in the box below.

$$\Delta DD = 1/r \times \Delta R$$

The expression (1/r), where r is the required reserve ratio, is known as the **deposit expansion multiplier**.

It is important to note that this multiple expansion of the money supply was a product of the actions of all the banks in the banking system. No single bank lent out more than its excess reserves.

Why did each bank restrict itself to lending out its excess reserves?—As a general rule, banks will limit their lending to no more than their excess reserves. Consider what could have happened if Bank A itself had based its lending on the deposit expansion multiplier formula and lent out $4,000.

Bank A

R 11,000	DD 55,000
L 94,000	NW 50,000

After the $4,000 had been spent and the check cleared, Bank A's balance sheet would have changed to:

Bank A

R 7,000	DD 51,000
L 94,000	NW 50,000

Bank A would no longer be meeting its required reserve ratio and would be in severe financial stress. It would also be subject to penalties imposed by the Federal Reserve System. This event can be avoided if banks restrict themselves to lending out no more than their excess reserves.

Real World Complications—In the real world, the deposit expansion multiplier is unlikely to be as large as the value given by the formula. There are three reasons for this:

1. Every bank holds some excess reserves.

2. Some of the new money created leaks out into cash and is not redeposited in a bank.

3. Some bank customers seek deposits other than checking accounts.

CHAPTER 13

MONETARY POLICY

13.1 THE FEDERAL RESERVE SYSTEM

The Federal Reserve System (known affectionately as the "Fed") is the central bank of the United States. Its responsibilities are to oversee the stability of the banking system and conduct monetary policy to the end of fighting inflation and unemployment and stimulating economic growth.

Structure—The Fed has an unusual structure. It consists of a Board of Governors, twelve regional banks, money subregional banks, and commercial banks that opt for membership in the system. Although created by an Act of Congress (in 1913), nominally the Fed is privately owned by the member banks. Members of the Board of Governors are appointed by the President and confirmed by the Senate for 14 year terms. The Chair of the Board is appointed by the President and confirmed by the Senate for a four year term. The Fed's budget is overseen by a committee of Congress and it must report to Congress about its operations at least twice a year. To a large extent, the Fed can be considered an independent agency of the government.

The Fed's virtual independence has led to a continuing controversy. Is it wise to give the power to influence the state of the economy to a group who are not directly accountable to the people? The "pro" side claims the Fed's independence puts it "above" politics and leads to decisions more in the "public interest." the "con" side says that in a democracy, the people should be given a voice in all decisions that affect them.

Functions—The major functions of the Fed are as follows:

1. **Bank Regulation**—The Fed has been given the responsibility of examining member banks to determine if they are financially strong and in conformity with the banking regulations. The Fed also approves mergers.

2. **Clearing Interbank Payments**—As shown in Chapter 12, the Fed performs a service for member banks in operating the check clearing function. Banks receiving deposit checks drawn on other banks can present them to the Fed. The Fed will credit the receiving bank's reserve account, reduce the paying bank's reserve account, and send the check back to the paying bank. Banks do not universally avail themselves of this service. Local banks will frequently cooperate and establish their own check clearing process for local checks.

3. **Lender of Last Resort**—One of the original motivations for establishing the Fed was to have a bank that could act as a "lender of last resort."

Bank panics refer to situations where depositors lose faith in their bank and try to withdraw their money. Given the fractional reserve nature of modern banking, it is impossible for all depositors to withdraw their money simultaneously. Failure of depositors to withdraw their money from one bank has the potential to scaring other depositors and starting a "run on the banks." By standing ready to loan reserves to banks experiencing difficulties, the Fed helps reduce the danger of panics.

Panics were much more common in the days before the Fed and **Federal Deposit Insurance,** but are not unknown today. Witness the situations with savings and loan institutions in Ohio and Maryland within the last few years.

FEDERAL DEPOSIT INSURANCE

Established during the New Deal era, Federal Deposit Insurance provides government guarantees for bank deposits should a bank fail. Both commercial banks and savings and loans are insured.

---

4. **Monetary Policy—**

a. **Open Market Operations**—Open market operations refers to the Fed's buying or selling of U.S. Government bonds in the open market. The purpose is to influence the amount of reserves in the banking system, and, consequently, the banking system's ability to extend credit and create money.

1. **To expand the economy**—The Fed would buy bonds in the open market. If $50 million in bonds was purchased directly from commercial banks, the banks' balance sheet would change as follows:

All Commercial Banks

R + 50 million	
Bonds − 50 million	

Banks are now holding an additional $50 million in excess

reserves which they can use to extend additional credit. To induce borrowers, banks are likely to lower interest rates and credit standards. As loans are made, the money supply will expand as explained in Chapter 12. The additional credit will stimulate additional spending, primarily for investment goods.

The $50 million in bonds could be purchased directly from private individuals. The private individuals would then deposit the proceeds in their bank accounts. After the money was deposited, the balance sheet of all commercial banks would look as follows:

All Commercial Banks

R	+ 50 million	DD	+ 50 million

As above, the banks are now holding excess reserves which they can use to extend credit. Lower interest rates, a greater money supply, and a higher level of total expenditure will result.

2. **To contract the economy**—The Fed would sell bonds in the open market. If it sold $20 million in bonds directly to the commercial banks, the banks' balance sheet would change as follows:

All Commercial Banks

R	− 20 million	
Bonds	+ 20 million	

Banks are now deficient in reserves. They need to reduce their demand deposit liabilities, and will do so by calling in loans and making new credit more difficult to get. Interest

A Primer on Bonds

Bonds are a financial instrument frequently used by government and business as a way to borrow money. Every bond comes with a par value (often $1000), a date to maturity (ranging from 90 days to 30 years), a coupon (a promise to pay a certain amount of money each year to the bondholder until maturity), and a promise to repay the par value on the maturity date. The issuing government or business sells the bonds in the bond market for a price determined by supply and demand. The money received from the sale represents the principal of the loan, the annual coupon payment is the interest on the loan, and the principal is repaid at the date of maturity. There is also a secondary market in bonds.

Assume a bond carries a coupon of $100 and is sold for $1000. Then the annual yield to the purchaser is roughly 10% ($100/$1000). If the same bond was sold for $950, the yield would be roughly 10.5% ($100/$950). If the same bond was sold for $1050, the yield would roughly be 9.5% ($100/$1050). Note the inverse relationship between bond yield and price. Also note that the actual yield formulas are considerably more complicated than those used.

rates will rise, credit requirements will be tightened, and the money supply will fall. Total spending in the economy will be reduced.

If the Fed sells the $20 million in bonds directly to private individuals, payment will be made with checks drawn against the private individuals' bank accounts. The banks' balance sheet will change as follows:

All Commercial Banks

R	− 20 million	DD	− 20 million

Again, banks are deficient in reserves. They are forced to reduce credit availability, which will raise interest rates, reduce the money supply, and lead to a drop in total spending.

b. **Reserve Ratio**—The Fed can set the legal reserve ratio for both member and non-member banks. The purpose is to influence the level of excess reserves in the banking system, and consequently, the banking system's ability to extend credit and create money.

1. **To expand the economy**—The Fed would reduce the reserve requirement. Assume the reserve requirement is 8%, and all banks are "all loaned up."

If the Fed reduces the reserve requirement to 6%, required reserves fall to $30 million, and there are immediately $10 million in excess reserves. Banks will lower the interest rates they charge and credit requirements in an attempt to make more loans. As the loans are granted, the economy's money supply and total spending will rise.

All Commercial Banks

R	40 million	DD	50 million

2. **To contract the economy**—The Fed would raise the reserve requirement. Assume the reserve requirement is 8%, and all banks are "all loaned up."

All Commercial Banks

R	40 million	DD	50 million

If the Fed raises the reserve requirement to 10%, required reserves rise to $50 million, and banks are immediately $10 million deficient in reserves. Banks will raise the interest rates they charge and credit requirements to reduce the amount of money borrowed. They may also call in loans. As the loans are reduced, the economy's money supply and total spending will fall.

c. **Discount Rate**—One of the responsibilities of the Fed is to act as a "lender of last resort." Member banks needing reserves can borrow from the Fed. The interest rate the Fed charges on these loans is called the **discount rate**. By changing the discount rate, the Fed can influence the amount member banks try to borrow, and, consequently, the banking system's ability to extend credit and create money.

1. **To expand the economy**—The Fed would lower the discount rate. A lower discount rate would make it less "painful" for member banks to borrow from the Fed. Consequently, they will be more willing to lend money and hold a low level of excess reserves. A lower discount rate would lead to lower interest rates and credit requirements, a higher money supply, and greater total spending in the economy.

2. **To contract the economy**—The Fed would raise the discount rate. A higher discount rate would make it more "painful" for member banks to borrow from the Fed. Consequently, they will be less willing to lend money and more likely to hold a high level of excess reserves. A higher discount rate would lead to higher interest rates and more stringent credit requirements, a lower money supply, and

lower total spending in the economy.

Monetary Policy Summary Table—

Tool	Action	Effect on Interest Rates	Effect on Money Supply	Effect on Total Spending	Effect on GNP
Open Market	buy	lower	raise	raise	raise
Operations	sell	raise	lower	lower	lower
Reserve	raise	raise	lower	lower	lower
Ratio	lower	lower	raise	raise	raise
Discount	raise	raise	lower	lower	lower
Rate	lower	lower	raise	raise	raise

13.2 THE DEMAND FOR MONEY

The convenience of money creates a demand for it. By this it is meant that households will choose to hold a certain portion of their wealth in money form. The convenience is primarily its liquidity (See 12.1). Money can be used to buy goods and services, acquire other assets, and provide a cushion against emergencies.

A household's demand for money is **positively related to its income** (households with higher incomes spend more money, and, consequently, need to hold more money to finance those transactions), and **negatively related to the interest rate** (higher interest rates [i.e. higher returns on assets other than money] increase the opportunity cost of holding wealth in money form because money typically pays no or very low interest).

The demand curve for money can be represented by D1. At higher levels of income, the demand curve will shift out to D2. At lower levels of income, the demand curve will shift in to D3.

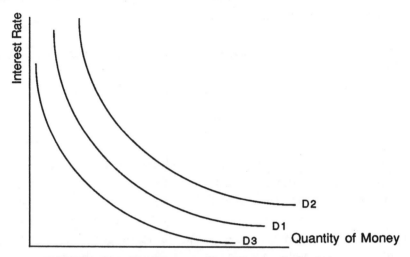

FIGURE 13.1–The Demand for Money Schedule

13.3 TRANSMISSION MECHANISM FOR MONETARY POLICY

Federal Reserve System actions influence the economy primarily by influencing interest rates, credit availability, and the money supply, and consequently, the interest rate sensitive portion of total spending (mainly, investment).

$$\uparrow MS \ \rightarrow \ \downarrow i \ \rightarrow \uparrow I \rightarrow \ \uparrow C + I + G + (X - M)$$

$$\downarrow MS \ \rightarrow \ \uparrow i \ \rightarrow \downarrow I \rightarrow \ \downarrow C + I + G + (X - M)$$

Graphically, an increase in the money supply from MS to MS′ will cause the equilibrium level of GNP to rise to GNP′. A decrease in the money supply from MS to MS″ will cause the equilibrium level of GNP to fall to GNP″.

13.4 MONETARISM

Monetarism is a school of thought within the economics profession. It is closely related to classical economics. The leading monetarist is Milton Friedman.

Equation of Exchange—The equation of exchange is written as

$$MV = PQ$$

where M = money supply, V = velocity of money (the rate at which money changes hands), P = the average price level, and Q = the quantity of goods and services. The equation says if you multiply the money supply by the rate at which money changes hands, you will get the value of goods and services sold (or the level of income, which is the same thing).

The equation exchange is true by definition. To see that, realize that three dollars in income is created if one dollar changes hands three times. Every time the dollar changes hands, a dollar in income will be created; so if you multiply the one dollar ($1) by the number of times it changes hands (3), you will get the amount of income created ($3).

Velocity of Money—As indicated above, the velocity of money measures the rate at which money changes hands. We cannot trace the movements of dollars in the economy the way we can trace birds by banding their legs, but we do not need to. Simple arithmetic shows that

$$V = \frac{PQ}{M}$$

Using available data on GNP ($4100 billion in 1988) and the money supply (M1 = $800 billion in 1988), the velocity of money was $4100/$800 = 5.125.

Quantity Theory of Money—The quantity theory of money was used by classical economists to explain the rate of inflation. From the equation of exchange, assume that V is constant due to institutional reasons, and Q is constant because the economy's equilibrium is at full employment. Then if M doubles, P must also double. Therefore, the price level is determined by the quantity of money.

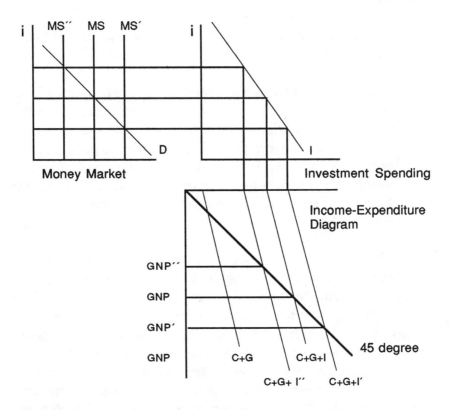

FIGURE 13.2–Effect of Changes in Money Supply on GNP

Tenets of Modern Monetarism—Modern day monetarists have modified the quantity theory of money. They recognize that Q may not be at the full employment level for extended periods of time. Also, they recognize that V is not a constant, but they believe that V is "relatively stable." This means that V does not change dramatically from year to year, and can be predicted with a relatively small margin of error. If so, then the money supply can be used to predict GNP (PQ) with a high degree of accuracy.

The most important beliefs of the modern monetarists are as follows:

1. Changes in the money supply are the most important factor affecting the economy.

2. The Fed should **not** use discretionary monetary policy in an attempt to stabilize the economy. This may seem contradictory with 1, but it really is not. The monetarists, as a rule, are economic conservatives. They believe the private sector of the economy tends to be relatively stable. Government actions are primarily to blame for economic difficulties. An activist monetary policy would create more problems that it would solve.

The reason for this is because monetary policy actions only affect the economy with a lag. The lag could be well over one year. Consequently, the only way the Fed could follow the appropriate policy today is if it were to know what the economy would be like in a year. Unfortunately, but truthfully, economists are not very apt at forecasting the economy. Thus the Fed is as likely to follow inappropriate policy as appropriate policy, as likely to make things worse as better. **The preferred approach of monetarists is for the Fed to let the money supply grow at a constant rate.** Since changes in the money supply are the main factor causing fluctuations in the economy, a smooth rate of growth for money should help smooth the growth of the economy. It is true that this policy will not permit the Fed to respond to major problems, but, again, the Fed's response is as likely to be bad as good. A constant rate of growth of the money supply is superior to any alternative.

CHAPTER 14

INFLATION

14.1 THEORY OF INFLATION

Demand Pull Inflation—"Too much money chasing too few goods" is an apt description of demand pull inflation. More technically, demand pull inflation occurs when the level of spending in the economy exceeds the amount firms are capable of producing. To ration the available goods and services, firms raise prices. Excess demand, then, pulls up the general price level.

In a simple Keynesian model, inflation is unlikely to occur when the economy is operating below full employment. If there is an increase in spending firms will hire unemployed resources and produce more output. Competition leads firms to respond with output increases rather than price increases. When the economy reaches full employment, firms no longer have the option of increasing output. They must raise prices. The solution to demand pull inflation is to reduce demand.

In Figure 14.1, an increase in aggregate expenditure from AE1 to AE2 will result in higher GNP with no increase in the

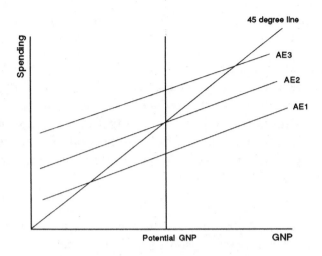

FIGURE 14.1–Demand-Pull Inflation

price level. A further increase to AE3 will only result in higher prices.

Phillips Curve—Named after Australian economist A.W. Phillips, the Phillips curve was originally a relationship between the level of unemployment and the rate of increase of wages. Since wage increases typically lead to price increases, a natural extension was to look at the relationship between the level of unemployment and the rate of inflation, and this latter

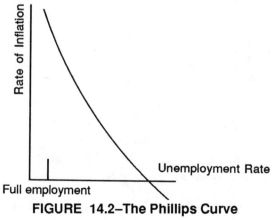

FIGURE 14.2–The Phillips Curve

136

relationship was what most economists mean today when they refer to the Phillips Curve.

There are two significant things about the Phillips Curve. First, it indicates that there is a **trade-off** between inflation and unemployment. Policies that reduce unemployment have a cost in terms of higher inflation. Policies to fight inflation have a cost in terms of higher unemployment. Second, it indicates that inflationary problems can begin before an economy reaches full employment.

An explanation for the second phenomenon is the sectoral inflation theory. According to this theory, as an economy expands out of a recession, some sectors of the economy (i.e. industries) will reach full capacity before others. The sectors at full capacities will be forced to raise prices if expansion continues, while other sectors continue to struggle with used capacity (unemployment). As more sectors reach full capacity (the economy gets nearer to full employment), the inflation rate will increase.

The Phillips Curve appeared a good description of the economy's behavior in the 1950's and 1960's. During the 1970's and 1980's it was not as good. Economists have speculated that

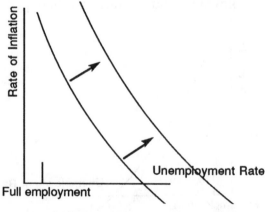

FIGURE 14.3–The Shifting Phillips Curve

the Phillips Curve is capable of shifting in or out and it shifted out during the last two decades, giving us a worsened trade-off.

Inflationary Expectations—Inflationary expectations refers to society's beliefs about what is going to happen to the rate of inflation. It is an important concept because inflationary expectations tend to be self-fulfilling. If consumers believe inflation will increase in the future, they are apt to buy more and save less now, contributing to excess demand. If workers believe that inflation is going to increase in the future, they are apt to demand automatic wage increases to protect them and have cost-of-living protections built into labor contracts. Both actions will raise future costs and make inflation more likely. Higher inflationary expectations will shift the Phillips Curve outward. Lower expectations will shift the curve inward. One important goal of economic policy becomes influencing people's expectations.

Accelerationist Hypothesis—Much of the economics profession today believes the long run Phillips Curve is a vertical line at the natural rate of unemployment. This implies there is no permanent trade-off between inflation and unemployment, and that full employment can be achieved and held at any level of inflation, provided people come to expect that rate and adjust accordingly.

Attempts to hold unemployment below the natural rate will lead to accelerating inflation. This is because policies which reduce unemployment (i.e. policies that increase aggregate expenditure) will raise prices and wages and throw markets out of equilibrium. As firms recognize their wage costs have risen, they will be forced to raise prices further. As workers realize the purchasing power of their higher wages has been reduced by higher prices, they will demand still greater wage increases. Inflationary expectations will take hold and wages and prices

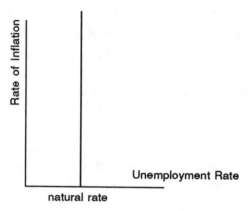

FIGURE 14.4–The Long Run Phillips Curve

push each other higher and higher. Only high unemployment for an extended period of time is capable to bringing the inflation rate back to an acceptable level.

Cost Push and Supply Shock Inflation—Both refer to similar situations, when factors on the supply side of the economy push up costs of production and force firms to raise prices. Cost push inflation is the term frequently used when labor unions are deemed the villians in the story. According to the theory, irresponsible unions demand and win "excessive" wage increases which force firms to raise prices. Of course, the price increases become the rationale for a new round of wage increases leading to a **wage-price spiral**. A variation on the story sees the initial push coming from firms that raise prices to raise their profits. These prices are costs to other firms and they also stimulate labor to demand higher wages, and the spiral continues. Supply Shock inflation is of more recent vintage. It occurs when a vital resource becomes scarce, causing its price to rise and raising costs of production for firms, setting off an upward spiral. An example of a factor causing supply shock inflation would be oil shortages. Both can be presented graphically by an outward shift of the Phillips Curve. Both create dilemmas for anti-inflation policy because upward movements in costs will also force firms to lay-off workers. Thus the economy faces stagflation. If the authorities raise demand to put people back to work, the inflation problem worsens. If the authorities reduce demand to fight inflation, the unemployment problem gets worse.

14.2 AGGREGATE DEMAND AND AGGREGATE SUPPLY MODEL

The simple Keynesian model as represented by the Income-Expenditure diagram is not adequate to explain the dynamics of inflation as the United States has experienced it over the last two decades. The Aggregate Demand and Aggregate Supply Model is more enlightening.

Aggregate Demand Schedule—The Aggregate Demand Schedule shows the relationship between the general price level and the real level of spending in the economy.

The negative relationship can be explained this way. A reduction in the general price level increases the real value of consumer wealth, leading to greater spending and hence a higher level of real GNP.

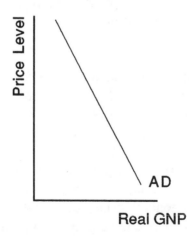

FIGURE 14.5–The Aggregate Demand Schedule

AD shifts in	AD shifts out
higher taxes on households	lower taxes on households
lower government spending	higher government spending
Fed reduces money supply	Fed increases money supply
reduced consumer confidence	increased consumer confidence
higher corporate taxes	lower corporate taxes

Table 14.1

As a general rule, only events that reduce aggregate expenditure shift the AD schedule in; any event that raises aggregate expenditure will shift AD out. Examples of events that will shift AD are shown in Table 14.1.

Aggregate Supply Schedule—The Aggregate Supply Schedule shows the relationship between the general price level and the amount of real output firms produce.

The positive relationship can be explained this way. A higher price level will stimulate greater production because it offers more opportunity for profit. Alternatively, since greater production will raise costs of production, firms must charge higher prices.

As a general rule, events that raise costs of production will shift AS inward; events reducing costs of production will shift AS outward. Examples of events that will shift AS are shown in Table 14.2.

Equilibrium in the Aggregate Demand/Aggregate Supply Model—The intersection of the AD and AS schedules gives the equilibrium general price level and real GNP. Shifts in either curve will change the equilibrium point.

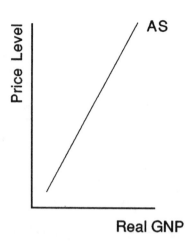

Price Level / **Real GNP** / **AS**

FIGURE 14.6–The Aggregate Supply Schedule

AS shifts in	AS shifts out
higher inflationary expectations	lower inflationary expectations
"excessive" wage increases	wage "give-backs"
higher taxes on business	lower taxes on business

Table 14.2

Using the Model—The model can be used to predict how the economy will react to various situations.

Increase in AD—Assume AD increases for some reason. Initially the level of real GNP and employment will rise along with the price level. This is the standard Phillips Curve relation. However, several things will happen next. As workers realize that prices have risen, they will demand wage increases to cover the increase in the price level. In addition, their inflationary expectations will increase. Also, firms will observe their costs of production going up both as a result of higher wages and higher material costs. This will cause the AS schedule to shift in. Prices will increase further and output (and employment) will fall unless the authorities react by increasing AD even more, which will cause prices to increase still more and

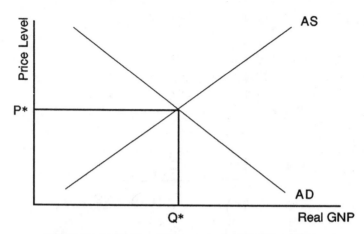

FIGURE 14.7–Equilibrium in AD/AS Model

create the conditions for another shift in the AS schedule.

Decreases in AS—Assume a supply shock, like an oil embargo. This will shift in the AS schedule leading to both higher prices and lower real GNP (and employment). If the authorities try to restore the lost jobs by raising AD, prices will go still higher. If the authorities try to reduce inflation, real GNP (and employment) will be further reduced.

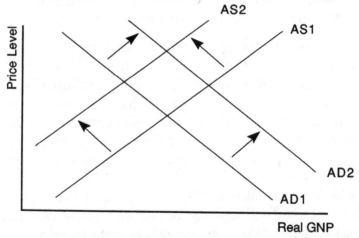

FIGURE 14.8–Increase in Aggregate Demand

14.3 ANTI-INFLATION POLICY

Reducing Aggregate Demand—Lowering the money supply or government spending or raising taxes is the classic solution to inflation. Given adequate time, it will always work. Unfortunately, the side effects are sometimes worse than the disease. Using the Phillips Curve idea, reductions in demand will inevitably cause job loses, possibly for extended periods of time if peoples' inflationary expectations take a while to adjust to the new environment. This policy is sometimes called "biting the bullet" or "the old-time religion."

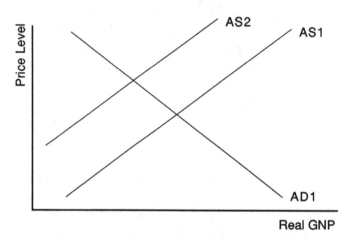

FIGURE 14.9–Decrease in Aggregate Supply

Rational Expectations—Rational expectations is a relatively new school of thought in the economics profession. It believes that people form inflationary expectations quickly in a rational manner, using all the information available. Its significance in this context is the theory's prediction that inflation is capable of being beaten quickly with limited cost. This will happen if the government has credibility with the public. Thus if the government proclaims an anti-inflationary policy, the public immediately believes it and adjusts its inflationary expectations immediately to an environment of no inflation. Under

144

these circumstances inflation will fall almost instantaneously, and there need be no extended period of high unemployment.

Wage and Price Controls—Economists who believe that inflationary problems stem largely from cost push factors are attracted to wage and price controls as a solution. Under this policy, government decrees limits on how much wages and prices can be raised. This will both directly reduce inflation and also reduce inflationary expectations. Conservative economists believe this cure is worse than the disease because the controls will distort markets, causing artificial shortages of goods and services. The United States has used controls during wartime fairly successfully. A full-fledged system of controls was in effect during part of the Nixon Administration. While the controls reduced inflation while they were in effect, many economists believe the post-controls price explosion meant they had no long term positive impact. A mild form of controls was used during the Kennedy-Johnson Administration. Wage and Price Controls are sometimes known as an **income policy**.

TIP—TIP stands for tax-based income policy. Its purpose is to use the tax system to control wages and prices. A common form is to offer tax reductions to groups of workers and firms who show restraint in their wage and price behavior.

CHAPTER 15

ECONOMIC GROWTH

15.1 FUNDAMENTALS OF ECONOMIC GROWTH

Productivity—Productivity is a measure of how much output we produce for each hour of work. If a worker is able to produce 10 widgets in an hour's time, then the worker's productivity is 10 widgets per hour. Productivity should not be confused with total output. The relationship between the two is that:

> Total Output = Productivity × Number of Hours Worked

If a worker produces 10 widgets per hour and works 40 hours, then total output is 10 widgets per hour × 40 hours = 400 widgets.

Productivity and Living Standards—The key to improving a nation's living standards is to raise productivity. If we can produce more per hour, then more is available to be consumed, we can work fewer hours, or some combination of the two.

Increasing Productivity—There are two main ways to raise productivity. **We can work harder, or we can work smarter.** Working harder refers to expending more effort during each hour of work. It seems unlikely that much of our economy's increase in productivity over time reflects people actually working harder. Working smarter refers to a number of factors, including using more and better capital equipment, better education, more finely developed job skills, and better health. Presumably the bulk of our increase in productivity reflects these factors.

Assume two farm workers are given the task of plowing a ten acre field. Farm worker 1 is given an ox and a plow. Farm worker 2 is given a modern tractor complete with air-conditioned cab and tape deck. It is obvious that 2 will be more productive, but it is unlikely that 2 will have worked "harder." Farm worker 2's higher productivity reflects the fact that she has more and better capital to work with and the skills to operate it.

Rule of 72—This is a mathematical rule of thumb that can be applied to growth rates. If you divide the growth rate of anything into 72, you get that approximate amount of time it takes for that thing to double in size.

Time to Double = 72/growth rate

For example, if real GNP grows 3% a year, then it should take approximately 72/3 = 24 years for GNP to double in size.

The rule of 72 is important in talking about productivity growth. From approximately the end of World War II to the late 60's, productivity grew about 3% per year in the United States.

Since that time, it has grown about 1% per year. A two percentage point difference might not seem like much, but if you apply the rule of 72 then the difference is seen to be highly significant. At a 3% growth rate, productivity will double every 24 years, about a generation. At a 1% growth rate, it will take 72 years for productivity to double, about the average life span of an individual. The change in productivity growth rates will cause dramatic differences in future living standards.

15.2 SUPPLY-SIDE ECONOMICS

Supply-side economics is an approach to economics that places great emphasis on the effect of policies on our willingness to work and ability to produce. In a sense, all economists are "supply-siders" because economic analysis has always stressed the influence of incentives in influencing both consumption and production behavior, but, in the context of the United States, supply-side economics usually refers to the policy views of a group of economists and politicians who have actively promoted above all else the use of tax cuts and deregulation as a method of restoring rapid growth. They believed that marginal tax rates were so high as to dramatically reduce the reward from working, saving, and investing with predictable undesirable results. Likewise, excessive government regulation of business was alleged to be stifling productive activity. These views were very prominent during the administration of President Ronald Reagan.

Laffer Curve—Associated with economist Arthur Laffer, the Laffer curve (See Figure 15.1) concept almost perfectly summarizes what supply-side economics is all about. The curve shows the relationship between the marginal tax rate and the government's tax revenue.

At a 0% tax rate, the government obviously will not take in

148

any revenue. At a 100% rate, the government likewise will not take in any revenue because there is no reward for working so no one will work and earn any income. Since the government does tax and take in some revenue, the curve must have a positively sloped segment, but it also must curve back at some tax rate to reach the point of 0 revenue and 100% tax rate.

While no economist would disagree with the basic logic of the Laffer curve, what supply-side economists did was to take the extra step to imply that American tax rates were so high that the economy was on the negatively sloped portion of the curve. They then advocated tax rate cuts as a way to stimulate higher productivity with the added bonus that the government's revenues would actually increase.

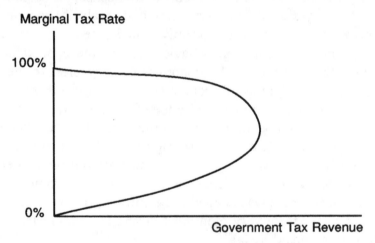

FIGURE 15.1–The Laffer Curve

CHAPTER 16

INTERNATIONAL ECONOMICS

16.1 INCOME-EXPENDITURE MODEL WITH FOREIGN SECTOR

In the income-expenditure model, international economic transactions affect the economy through their influence on aggregate expenditure. Exports of goods and services represent foreign demand for our output, and add to aggregate expenditure. Imports of goods and services represent a diversion of domestic purchasing power to foreign product. Imports, then, are associated with a reduction in aggregate expenditure. A term representing net exports $(X - M)$ is added to the expression for aggregate expenditure.

$$AE = C + I + G (X - M)$$

This simple model ignores international transactions in real and financial assets.

Marginal Propensity to Import—Imports are considered to be induced spending. The level of imports is influenced positively by household income. As household income rises, households buy more goods and services, including those produced in foreign countries. The marginal propensity to import measures the proportion of additional income spent on imports.

$$MPM = \Delta M / \Delta DI$$

Export Multiplier—The export multiplier measures the change in GNP resulting from a $1 change in exports.

$$\text{Export Multiplier} = \Delta GNP / \Delta X$$

The formula is:

$$\text{Export Multiplier} = 1/(1 - MPC + MPM)$$

Impact on other multipliers—Recognition of the foreign sector causes the formulas for the other autonomous expenditure multipliers to be modified.

$$\text{Consumption multiplier} = 1/ (1 - MPC + MPM)$$

$$\text{Investment multiplier} = 1/ (1 - MPC + MPM)$$

$$\text{Government spending multiplier} = 1/ (1 - MPC + MPM)$$

$$\text{Tax multiplier} = (MPM - MPC)/ (1 - MPC + MPM)$$

16.2 INTERNATIONAL TRADE

Why do nations trade with each other?

Principle of Absolute Advantage—A country possesses an absolute advantage in the production of a good or service if it is the most efficient producer of the item. For example, since herring only swim in cold waters and bananas can only grow in warm, moist climates, Norway has an absolute advantage in fishing for herring and Guatamala has an absolute advantage in growing bananas. Norway is better off by devoting resources to fishing and using the herring caught to trade for Guatemalan bananas than trying to grow bananas itself. Likewise with Guatemala.

Law of Comparative Advantage—The law of comparative advantage explains why trade is beneficial between two nations even if one of the nations holds an absolute advantage in the production of all goods and services. In other words, absolute advantage is irrelevant to explaining the pattern of specialization and trade.

Assume a world of two nations of about equal size, called Japan and the United States. They are each capable of producing only two goods, telephones and VCRs. Resources are fully employed in both nations. The table shows total productivity in the production of both goods.

	Telephones per unit of resources	VCRs per unit of resources
Japan	2	6
U.S.	1	1

Note that Japan has an absolute advantage in the production of both goods. Note also the opportunity costs of production in both countries.

	Cost of One Telephone	Cost of One VCR
Japan	3 VCRs	1/3 telephone
U.S.	1 VCR	1 telephone

Opportunity costs are computed as follows. In Japan, if one unit of resources is shifted from VCR to telephone production, 6 VCRs must be given up to get 2 telephones. Therefore, 2 T = 6 VCR, or 1 T = 3 VCR. The opportunity cost of good X in terms of good Y is

> Y per unit of resources/ X per unit of resources

A country has a comparative advantage in the production of a good if it has the lowest opportunity cost. Here Japan has the comparative advantage in VCRs because they cost only 1/3 telephone as compared to 1 telephone in the United States. The U.S., despite being less efficient than Japan in telephone production, has a comparative advantage because telephones cost only 1 VCR as opposed to 3 in Japan. As a general rule, regardless of how inefficient a producer a country is, it is bound to have a comparative advantage in something.

Why and what will the Japanese trade with the United States? If the Japanese try to produce telephones, it will cost them 3 VCRs for every unit of resources shifted to telephone production. It may be cheaper to buy phones in the U.S. where they cost only 1 VCR. Similarly, domestically produced VCRs cost 1 telephone in the U.S., but the U.S. may be able to buy them cheaper in Japan, where they only cost 1/3 VCR. Even though Japan has an absolute advantage in the production of telephones, it makes sense form them to buy from the United States. Even though the U.S. lacks an absolute advantage in telephone production, it can be a successful competitor in the world market.

The magnitude of the gains from trade will depend on the world prices that arise for VCRs and telephones. The U.S. may charge Japan more than 1 VCR per phone. As long as the price is less than 3 VCRs, the Japanese are better off trading for phones than producing them themselves. Likewise with the U.S. and VCRs.

The price of phones and VCRs in the world market (the exchange ratio between phones and VCRs) cannot be determined precisely. We know it must be between 1T = 1VCR and 1T = 3VCR for both countries to be able to benefit from trade.

Regardless of the countless complications that could be added to this model, the lesson of the law of comparative advantage continues to hold.

Gains from specialization—An implication of the law of comparative advantage is that the gains to a nation from specializing and trading exceed the losses. Assume the tables show some of the points on the production possibilities curves for Japan and the United States.

United States

VCRs	30	27	24	21	18	15	12	9	6	3	0
Tele	0	3	6	9	12	15	18	21	24	27	30

Japan

VCRs	100	90	80	70	60	50	40	30	20	10	0
Tele	0	3.3	6.6	10	13.3	16.6	20	23.3	26.6	30	33.3

Graphs of each country's production possibilities curve are shown below:

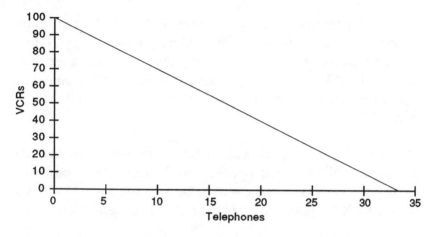

FIGURE 16.1–Japan's Production Possibilities Curve

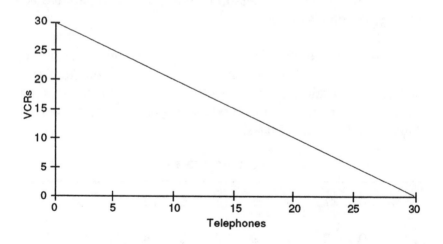

FIGURE 16.2–United States' Production Possibilities Curve

If both countries try to be self-sufficient and neither trades, the production possibility curves are also their consumption possibilities curves.

Assume now that trade opens up between Japan and the United States, and the world exchange ratio is 1 Telephone = 2 VCR. If Japan specialized in VCR production (producing 100), it could trade VCRs for as many as 50 telephones. This gives Japan's trading possibilities curve (see Table 16.3 and Figure 16.3). The U.S. could produce 30 phones if it specialized, but could trade for up to 60 VCRs (see Table 16.4 and Figure 16.4).

Japan's Trading Possibilities Curve

VCRs	100	90	80	70	60	50	40	30	20	10	0
Tele	0	5	10	15	20	25	30	35	40	45	59

United States' Trading Possibilities Curve

VCRs	60	54	48	42	36	30	24	18	12	6	0
Tele	0	3	6	9	12	15	18	21	24	27	30

The Interpretation of the Schedules–If Japan specialized in VCR production, it could product 100 units. If it kept them all to itself, it would consume 100 VCRs, but no telephones. If it traded 10 VCRs to the U.S., it would receive 5 telephones in return (at the exchange rate of 1T = 2VCR), allowing it to consume 90 VCRs and 5 telephones.

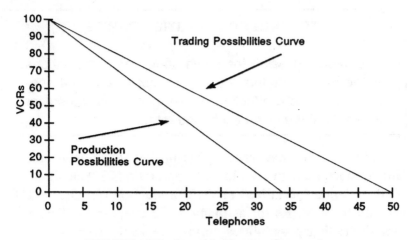

FIGURE 16.3–Japan's Production and Trading Possibilities Curve

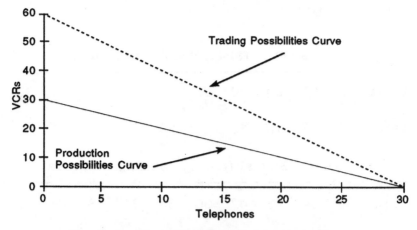

FIGURE 16.4–United States' Production and Trading Possibilities Curve

With specialization and trade, the trading possibilities becomes the new consumption possibilities curve.

Note the increased quantities of both goods that can be consumed, implying that each nation's overall standard of living will rise as a result of specialization and trade.

While some individuals may suffer from trade (telephone producers in Japan and VCR producers in the U.S.), the nation as a whole benefits (and the afflicted producers will be able to find jobs in the expanding sectors of their economies.)

Tariffs, Quotas, and other restrictions on trade—A tariff is a tax applied to an imported good. Its effect is to raise the good's price. A quota is a limitation on the amount of a good that can be imported. Its effect is also to raise the good's price. Both tariffs and quotas make foreign goods less competitive with domestic products, hurting foreign producers while protecting domestic producers. The law of comparative advantage implies that any restrictions on trade will be harmful to a nation because it will limit the degree of specialization and hence the gains described above.

Common Arguments made in favor of restriction on trade—

Cheap Foreign Wages—It is frequently asserted that low foreign wages enable foreign industries to out-compete domestic industries. The inevitable result is that domestic producers will be forced out of business, American workers will lose jobs, and our standard of living will fall (to the level of the foreigners!). Consequently we need to provide protection for American industries.

The argument is almost wholly fallacious. The absolute level

158

of wages is not what determines how competitive an industry is. Rather, it is the level of wages relative to the productivity of workers. If an American industry has high wages, but equally high productivity, it may very well be quite competitive with its foreign counterparts. In fact, it is high wage American industries that are some of our best performers in the international marketplace. The grain of truth in the argument is that some low wage foreign industries may, in fact, out-compete American industries, but this simply means that is where their comparative advantage lies and ours does not.

Infant Industry—The infant industry argument says that some new industries need time to develop the skills, techniques and efficiency necessary to be "world-class." Failure to protect these industries will lead to their being "snuffed-out" before they had a fair chance. Protection of selected industries is alleged to be behind the rise to prominence of Japan, Taiwan, South Korea, and Singapore, and is a significant part of the case made for industrial policy. The argument is valid as far as it goes, but it does not explain how a country is able to separate the "winners" from the "losers." Some economists feel that what will happen in practice is that politically influential but senile industries will end up being protected.

Terms of Trade—There are certain conditions (whose description must await more advanced courses) where a country may benefit at the expense of others by using tariffs. However, these conditions do not always exist, and countries must be prepared for the imposition of retaliatory tariffs, which end up making everyone worse-off.

Antidumping—There is widespread belief that some foreign governments subsidize their industries to allow them to sell below cost (dump) in the United States. American industries are said to be victims of "unfair competition." What is

159

seldom explained is why Americans should be upset if foreign governments help us buy products at low prices.

National Defense—The necessity of maintaining particular industries for national defense is often used as an argument to support protectionism. Like the infant industry argument, it is not illogical and cannot be completely evaluated in economic terms. Also like the infant industry argument, it suffers from the practical problem of how to identify those industries that are absolutely vital.

16.3 INTERNATIONAL FINANCE

How International Payments are Made—Buying goods, services, or assets from foreign countries is complicated by the fact that countries use different currencies. In the figure below, assume the American consumer wants to buy something sold by the German producer. The German producer would be unwilling to accept American dollars in exchange for the product because American dollars are worth nothing in Germany. The company cannot pay its workers, supplies, or shareholders in that currency. In order for the exchange to take place, there must be some way to change dollars into German marks.

Banks play a crucial role as traders of currency. Americans can take dollars to the bank and exchange them for marks. Germans can take marks to the bank and exchange them for dollars. Since banks trade both ways, taking dollars for marks and marks for dollars, they are able to maintain reserves of both currencies, unless a persistent trade imbalance forces holdings of one currency down to zero. In the diagram (Figure 16.5), German consumers and American producers also rely on banks to provide the necessary currency trading services.

The buying and selling of foreign currencies is what is

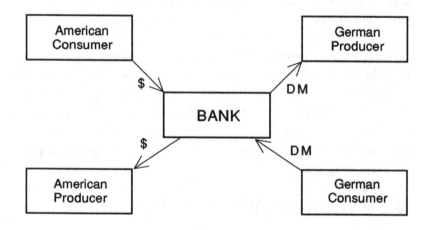

FIGURE 16.5–Making International Payments

meant by the foreign exchange market. Its participants include banks and other financial intermediaries, consumers, business firms, and governments.

(Actually, international financial transactions can be a lot more complicated than the figure shows. For many years the dollar has held a special place in the world financial system as a "key" currency. This means that foreign countries have had such faith in the dollar that they have frequently conducted transactions in dollars rather than their own national currencies.)

Exchange Rate—The exchange rate is simply the price of one nation's currency in terms of another's. The table shows exchange rates existing between the U.S. dollar and selected other currencies on May 9, 1989. For example, $1 buys 2.158 Dutch gilders, therefore 1 gilder buys $.4639. A product costing $25.00 in the U.S. would cost 53.95 gilders; a product costing 100 gilders would cost $46.39. (This ignores transportation and transaction costs.)

Selected Exchange Rates, May 9, 1989

$1.00 = .6017 British pounds	1 pound = $1.662
$1.00 = 6.4615 French francs	1 franc = $.1548
$1.00 = 2.158 Dutch gilders	1 gilder = $.4639
$1.00 = 134.85 Japanese yen	1 yen = $.007416
$1.00 = 1.9153 German marks	1 mark = $.5221
$1.00 = 2433 Mexican pesos	1 peso = $.000409
$1.00 = 1.1864 Canadian dollars	1 dollar = $.8429

Exchange Rate Appreciation—If the dollar/gilder rate changes to $1 = 2.25 gilders, we say the dollar has appreciated. Each dollar will buy more gilders. The dollar has become more valuable.

Exchange Rate Depreciation—In the above situation, the gilder depreciated because each gilder will now buy fewer dollars than before.

Balance of Payments—The balance of payments is a summary statement of the transactions that take place between a country and the rest of the world during a given period of time.

The balance of payments uses a double-entry system of bookkeeping. Transactions are recorded as debits and credits. From the standpoint of the U.S., a debit transaction is one that requires us to supply dollars. Examples of debit transactions are:

1. Imports of goods and services.

2. Gifts made to foreigners (also known as unilateral transfers).

3. Acquisition of a long term asset or reduction of a long

term liability (e.g. stocks, bonds, real capital).

4. Acquisition of a short term asset or reduction of a short-term liability (e.g. checking account balances or short term bonds).

From the standpoint of the U.S., a credit transaction is one that causes foreigners to demand dollars. Examples of credit transactions are:

1. Exports of goods and services.

2. Gifts received from foreigners.

3. Sale of a long term asset or long term liability increased.

4. Sale of a short term asset or short term liability incurred.

All transactions are placed into specific categories. The simplest breakdown is between the current account and the capital account. The current account records all transactions involving goods and services. The capital account records all transactions

	Debit	Credit
Current Account		
Capital Account		

TABLE 16.5–Schematic of the Balance of Payments Account

involving short and long-term assets. The balance of payment can be visualized as in Table 16.5.

The beginning of wisdom regarding the balance of payments is to realize that **every transaction gives rise to both debit and credit entries**. Consequently, the balance of payments must always balance in an accounting sense. For example,

1. Americans buy $800,000 in automobiles from Germany, paying for them with dollar checks drawn on American banks. The import of goods leads to a $800,000 debit in the current account. The German acquisition of dollar demand deposits increases our short term liabilities and results in a credit of $800,000 to the capital account.

2. The French buy the equivalent of $2,000,000 in private American corporation bonds, paying for them with franc checks. The sale of the bonds (long-term assets) leads to a $2,000,000 credit in the capital account. The acquisition of francs (short-term assets) leads to a $2,000,000 debit in the capital account.

3. American tourists travel in Holland, spending the equivalent of $5,000 on souvenirs. The gilders spent were obtained by exchanging dollars at a Dutch bank. The souvenirs are an import resulting in a $5,000 debit in the current account. The Dutch have acquired dollars, leading to a $5,000 credit in the capital account.

If we sum all debits and credits, both sides will be equal.

Balance of Payments "Imbalances"—Balance of payments "imbalances" result from looking at just a portion of the ledger.

1. **Balance of Trade**—The net balance of debits and credits for goods.

2. **Balance on Current Account**—The net balance of debits and credits for goods and services.

3. **Balance on Capital Account**—The net balance of debits and credits for short and long term assets.

Exchange Rate Determination —Exchange rates are set in the foreign exchange market by the forces of demand and supply.

Demand Curve for Dollars—If the Dutch want to acquire our goods, services, and assets, they must acquire dollars. This is the basis of the demand curve for dollars. The more valuable the gilder, the greater the quantity demanded of dollars because a valuable gilder makes American goods, services, and assets a better buy to the Dutch.

Supply Curve of Dollars—If Americans want to acquire Dutch goods, services, and assets, they must acquire gilders. To do so, they must supply dollars, Here, the more valuable the dollar, the greater the quantity supplied. (More advanced treatments allow the supply curve to have a negative slope in some cases.)

Equilibrium—At the exchange rate of $1 = 2.25 gilders, the strength of the American dollar makes Dutch goods, services, and assets a good buy for Americans. The weakness of the gilder makes American goods, services, and assets less attractive to the Dutch. Consequently, there is an excess supply of dollars and that will drive down the exchange rate.

At the exchange rate $1 = 1.75 gilders, the weakness of the dollar makes Dutch goods, services, and assets a bad buy for Americans. The strength of the gilder makes American goods services and assets more attractive to the Dutch. Consequently, there is an excess demand for dollars and that will drive up the exchange rate.

At the exchange rate $1 = 2 gilders, quantity demanded equals quantity supplied and the market is in equilibrium.

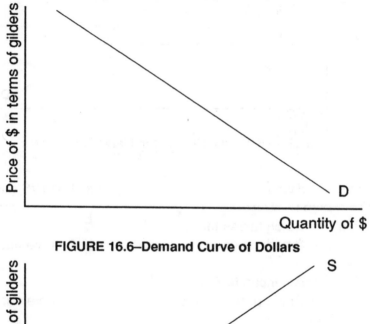

FIGURE 16.6–Demand Curve of Dollars

FIGURE 16.7–Supply Curve of Dollars

Shifts in the Curves—The foreign exchange market is unique in that frequently events can cause both curves to shift.

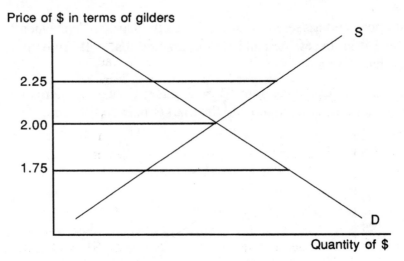

FIGURE 16.8–Equilibrium in the Market for Dollars

Factor	Event	Effect on D/S curve
Tastes	Dutch tastes for American goods increases	shift D curve out
	American tastes for Dutch goods increases	shift S curve out
Income	American income increases	shift S curve out
	Dutch income decreases	shift D curve in
Interest Rates	American rates increase	S shifts out D shifts out
Inflation	Higher inflation in U.S. than Holland	S shifts out D shifts in

Purchasing Power Parity Doctrine—The purchasing power parity doctrine (PPP) says exchange rates will adjust to equalize the purchasing power of a unit of currency in all countries. For example, assume perfume sells for $20 a bottle in the U.S. and 50 gilders a bottle in Holland. PPP says the exchange rate will adjust to $1 = 2.5 gilders, so that both Americans and the Dutch are indifferent between buying the perfume in America or Holland. If the exchange rate was $1 = 3 gilders, perfume in Holland would cost Americans $16.67 and perfume in America would cost the Dutch 60 gilders. This would lead both countries to buy perfume in Holland the the gilder would appreciate in value. If the exchange rate was $1 = 2 gilders, perfume would be cheaper in America (can you calculate the price in gilders?). The demand for dollars would cause the dollar to appreciate. The only equilibrium is at PPP.

Exchange Rate Regimes—Exchange rate regimes refers to the system by which exchange rates are set.

Floating (Flexible) Exchange Rates—Under this system, exchange rates are solely determined by the market. The major advantage is that the market will automatically bring the flows of currency into equilibrium. If there is an excess supply of dollars (meaning foreign goods, services, and assets are relatively more attractive), the dollar will depreciate making these goods, services and assets more expensive and reducing the quantity demanded.

Criticisms include:

1. Exchange rates become unpredictable, increasing the risk element involved in international trade.

2. Speculators will have to much influence on the market.

Fixed Exchange Rates—Under a fixed exchange rate system, every country sets the value of its currency in terms of every other one and pledges to take steps to maintain that exchange rate. For example, assume the U.S. dollar/British pound rate is set at ER1, but an increase in the demand for dollars (from D to D´) puts upward pressure on the rate. Either the U.S. or British government then must enter the market and supply enough dollars (Q2 − Q1) to keep the exchange rate at ER1.

The excess demand for dollars is frequently called the British balance of payments "deficit." This situation is a balance of payments "surplus" for the United States.

The major advantage of fixed exchange rates is that the future value of the exchange rate is known with certainty so that there is less risk associated with international trade.

The major disadvantage is that the exchange rate set may become "unrealistic," leading to persistent balance of payments deficits or surpluses. Deficits are the bigger problem.

In the example, if the British run persistent deficits at ER1:

a) If the British take responsibility for maintaining the exchange rate, they may eventually run out of dollars. Further, the dollars supplied may fuel inflation in the United States.

b) If the U.S. takes responsibility for maintaining the exchange rate, the dollars supplied may lead to domestic inflation.

Countries with persistent deficits may do several things:

1. Domestic economic policy may become "captive" to

Price of $ in terms of pounds

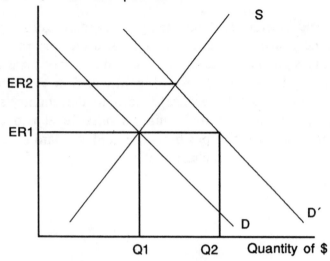

FIGURE 16.9–Fixed Exchange Rates

international concerns. A balance of payments deficit may force a country to raise domestic interest rates or reduce domestic income to decrease the demand for foreign goods, services, and assets.

2. There may be pressure for protectionism to stop the deficit.

3. The deficit country may be forced to "devalue" its currency. In the example, the British may give up on ER1 and begin supporting ER2. Devaluation may be the indicated policy in this case, but it is always a blow to national pride, and is contrary to what the system of fixed exchange rates is trying to accomplish.

"Dirty" Float—The current U.S. exchange rate system can be described as a "dirty" float. The exchange rate is allowed to be set by the market, but the government is prepared to intervene if the exchange rate gets "too far out of line."

Gold Standard—Under the gold standard, gold is the internationally accepted currency and is used for trade. If one country's goods, services, and assets are deemed especially desirable by the rest of the world, gold will flow to that country. The influx of gold, because it adds to the country's money supply, will increase the country's price level and erode its favorable competitive position. The gold standard is equivalent to a system of fixed exchange rates.